HOW TO PLAY THE PIANO

FOR BEGINNERS

Copyright © 2019 Tony R. Smith All Rights Reserved.

No part of this publication may be reproduced, distributed, or transmitted in any form or by any means, including photocopying, recording, or other electronic or mechanical methods, or by any information storage and retrieval system without the prior written permission of Smith Show Publishing, except in the case of very brief quotations embodied in critical reviews and certain other noncommercial uses permitted by copyright law.

TABLE OF CONTENTS

INTRODUCTION..3

Chapter one 6

  Learning How to Play the Piano for Beginners 6

  Beginner Piano Lessons - Get Started on How to Play the Piano 9

  Regular Mistakes When Learning How to Play the Piano......15

  Piano For Beginners Guide..19

  Piano For Beginners 27

  Digital Piano Keyboards 30

Chapter two 38

  7 Reasons Why Digital Piano Keyboards Make Great Gifts 38

  Eight Precious Tips to Help You Learn Piano by Yourself.......42

  Ten Reasons to Get Those Ten Fingers Playing Piano............48

  Learn to Play Piano - Left-Hand Playing Is The Reverse of Right-Hand Playing...55

  How to Play Piano - Playing With Both Hands Simultaneously 65

  Bonus Section Facts about Famous Musicians......................73

Conclusion..101

INTRODUCTION

If you are thinking about how to play the piano for beginners, well don't stress since it is simple. The initial step is deciding to learn, and once you have made the responsibility and have the first inspiration, then the rest will pursue. Before long you will never again be a beginner!

In case you have never played the piano, or are merely thinking about how to play the piano for beginners, at that point you are likely pondering precisely how to begin. Beginning something new and complex, for example, learning the piano may appear to be overwhelming at first, and you may not realize where to start. Indeed, deciding to attempt this astounding errand is your first assignment, so congrats to you on the start of your new voyage. It won't be simple, yet it tends to be fun and incredibly compensating as long as you stay with it.

As a beginner attempting to choose how best to approach this, you need to settle on some essential choices. You need to decide on private courses and online courses; you need to choose how much time you need to put into this new pastime, and how a lot of cash you need to spend.

This last choice is most likely one of the hardest. Money is frequently a deciding variable in numerous things. You might think about whether you can even bear to do this by any means. Indeed, you can! In this day and age, there are incredibly high-quality online courses for not precisely 50% of what you would pay for a month of private lessons. You can likewise learn in the solace of your own home and voluntarily. You can invest as much energy as you need learning and rehearsing, and go at your very own pace. You will be astonished at how rapidly and effectively you can learn.

Beginner piano players need to go gradual at first. Make yourself remarkably OK with the piano before you continue. Invest some energy playing the keys, playing with your fingers and discovering what the piano sounds like. Your lessons will show you legitimate fingering and appropriate harmonies, however before you even start taking some time becoming accustomed to the keyboard with no specific angles. Begin by having a fabulous time! Keep an inspirational frame of mind towards your voyage.

Anybody can have a terrible day. Try not to get excessively disappointed, take breaks when you believe you need them and on the off chance that you are feeling particularly great one day, at that point complete somewhat additional. Reward yourself when you have an accomplishment, and above all appreciate the procedure!

If you are considering how to play the piano for beginners, don't be anxious! Playing the keyboard is a lovely, mysterious thing, and best of everything it tends to be finished by completely anyone! There are incredible online projects made by experts that contrast with private lessons that won't tear an opening in your pocket. Projects like these are more adaptable than usual ones and will make them learn in no time.

CHAPTER ONE

Learning How to Play the Piano for Beginners

A few sites that furnish many hopeful piano players with step by step guidelines on piano lessons exist today. This methods for learning how to play the piano for beginners could be a delightful affair that empowers any beginner to esteem a wide range of music. The majority of the keyboard for beginners' lessons does not assume any prior learning of the piano.

Most of grand piano for beginners' lessons will have these components: a presentation, which presents the methods for learning how to play the piano, some basic notes which ought to be perused, just as learning some basic mood and in conclusion, participating in middle of the road lessons. These locales, made explicitly for piano beginners, should only be taken as a fundamental guide to learning how to play the piano. They ought not to be utilized as the primary wellspring of piano for the beginners learning process.

For what reason is the piano widely utilized in western music? This is such a result of the instrument's adaptability notwithstanding having the capacity to be used in various musical circumstances. In this way, as a beginner, it is vital to approach or possess a piano, regardless of whether it is the costly top notch amazing piano or an electronic keyboard or a minimal effort upright piano. The electronic keyboard and a minimal effort upright piano is ordinarily utilized in piano for beginners' classes since they are moderately low-valued and straightforward to use.

The following are a few steps that are intended to give you the piano for beginners' nuts and bolts of playing the piano. The initial phase would acquaint oneself with some critical parts of a piano before starting to play. These parts include: a Keyboard, which denotes the level line of keys that are utilized by piano player to produce sound; Keys, which are single units that must be pushed down in order to play notes; Pedals, which are used to change just as support, the tonal nature of the played notes; and a Music Rack that is being used in holding your guidance manual, or sheet music, or some other type of guide that you can allude to as you practice.

The second step would include acing the terms utilized, for example, Pitch, which is typically used to allude to the height or lowness of the sound of a note, just as Octave, which musically offers reference to a twelve key interim between two signs having comparable musical esteem.

The third step includes perusing diverse kinds of music as you practice with your fingers. This being your first piano for beginners' keyboard lesson, the first finger practices must be genuinely uncomplicated just as not being excessively marvelous. At this stage, you won't be required to sound like an expert or an experienced piano player. This step, in this straightforward piano for beginners' guide, was structured with the target of concentrating on keeping your hands, wrists just as fingers in great structure, and having the capacity to play the resulting practices effectively. Since it is hard to work one bicep in confinement, endeavor to show the left hand whatever the right side does.

Beginner Piano Lessons - Get Started on How to Play the Piano

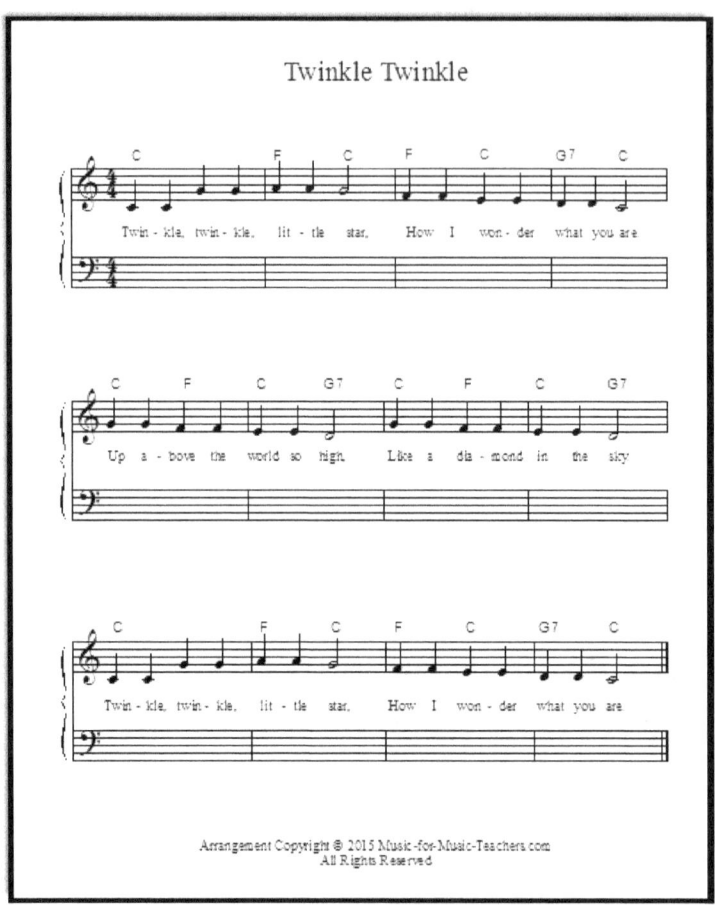

To begin with beginner piano lessons, you first need to realize the nuts and bolts before experiencing every one of the subjects on piano lesson books. Since you will show yourself how to play the piano, it will be essential to assimilate these lessons as these will establish the necessary framework on how you can turn into a specialist musician.

Before you can even play the piano by contacting the keyboard, you should figure out how to sit appropriately at the piano seat. The right stance is indispensable so a beginner should know this for that person to most likely conclusively and serenely play the piano.

There is additionally the correct method for playing the piano keyboard. The right situating of the hands, wrist, and fingers is necessary with the goal that you can play at a casual position, and you can keep away from any piano-related damage over the long haul. If you don't gain proficiency with this suitably, you will likewise danger of building unfortunate propensities in piano playing that will similarly be hard to change later on.

For a beginner, we see the long piano keys can be overpowering. Knowing the design of the piano keys at first by learning the rehashed examples of white and dark piano keys can make things straightforward.

To probably play quick and simple, playing with harmonies is the best approach. By learning the piano harmonies, like guitar playing, you can start playing any songs that you need. The trouble will rely upon the sort of balances that a song has.

These are the underlying starting piano lessons. For you to adapt effectively, you have to pursue the steps on these lessons accurately so you can go to further advanced experiences in a breeze.

Piano for Beginners - Learn How to Play the Piano

There are numerous routes for you to become familiar with the essentials of playing the piano and one of them is by searching for accommodating references that include a keyboard for beginners. Learning how to play the piano requires some serious energy and exertion. There is a lot of things that you need to adapt, for example, the notes, keys, the G-clef and the F-clef, pads, and sharps and other details. While it might appear to be confounded, there are routes for you to jumpstart learning.

You can ask somebody you know, similar to a companion or a relative, to show you how to peruse the notes in musical compositions. It is essential for you to understand the places of each, so you will know which piano key to play. For example, you need to know which piano key is DO, which is RE, which is MI, etc. Acquainting yourself with the piano keys is essential to play a musical tune.

You additionally need to gain proficiency with the distinctive sorts of notes and their span to play a song effectively. You need to realize what an entire sign looks like and to what extent it must be performed; the equivalent goes for other notes - the half note, quarter note, etc. The letters make the song and the beat of each musical piece.

If you find a book or whatever another reference that highlights piano for beginners, you will have a thought on the most proficient method to position your hands on the piano keyboard and how to play original tunes. You can start from that point and afterward bit by bit advancement as you ace every essential system. Take as much time as is needed in learning how each note and key is played. As you turn out to be increasingly more comfortable with the places of each letter, you turn out to be better in perusing and playing other musical compositions for piano.

You can look online for essential lessons in piano for beginners. Learning how to play the keyboard starts with some necessary data, and after that, it goes from that point. Your dimension of enthusiasm regarding the matter just as your musical tendency can enable you to jumpstart learning even without anyone else's input. It takes a ton of tolerance and system.

When you gain proficiency with the different musical notes and how they are played on the piano, you can concoct your unique piano methods. Try not to overpower yourself with bunches of data and different details. There are two or three things that you will learn as you come and afterward everything will only stream in.

Piano for beginners, Basic Piano Lessons, and other comparable references can enable you to assemble the essential establishment you have to play the piano. Take as much time as is needed, be patient and play from the heart. In no time, you will most likely make delightful music.

Regular Mistakes When Learning How to Play the Piano

Except if you have an exceptionally skillful educator helping you figure out how to play the piano, it can sometimes be troublesome as a piano beginner to know whether you are doing things right or not. To enable you to comprehend in case you're progressing nicely, beneath you'll find a rundown of the most popular mistakes made by beginners when learning how to play the piano.

#1. You need to play everything quick. Consider it for a second. OK show your kid how to keep running before the person in question can even walk? No. The equivalent runs with playing the piano. There is positively nothing worth mentioning that can turn out from endeavoring to play everything quickly from the get-go. An excessive number of piano beginners open a book and attempt to play the song as quick as they believe suitable from the first attempt. Without a doubt enough, they will in all probability make a couple of mistakes. They will at that point start over from the earliest starting point and attempt to play it again without backing off. By doing this, you will never address the mistakes or even have the capacity to experience the harder sections legitimately.
The standard guideline when learning piano? Moderate down!

#2. At whatever point you get familiar with another song, you endeavor to play the entire thing immediately. Once more, you may believe you're gainful by playing the whole song on the first attempt, yet you truly aren't helping yourself out like this. A decent correlation would be the 'steak' similarity. You can't eat an entire piece of steak in one chomp. You can't play an entire piece flawlessly in one attempt either. Rather, go one nibble at a time and separate the songs into sections. You may find that a few sections are simpler than others while some are progressively troublesome; take a shot at those troublesome sections to coordinate them with the less demanding parts rather than continually playing the entire song from the earliest starting point. Same goes when you make a mistake: rather than returning to the start and seeking after the best at whatever point you get to that entry, work through it gradually until you are alright with it. At exactly that point would you be able to return to the start with the conviction that you'll have the capacity to play through that entry!

#3. You think rehearsing 2 hours today will make up for not repeating for a couple of days. When learning anything new, the key is consistency. Piano beginners will regularly take a seat for a couple of hours one day, wholly retained in their learning, yet will, therefore 'overlook' to practice for whatever remains of the week. This won't support you; quality practice time isn't an aggregation of how long you practiced inside the multi-week, yet rather how regularly you sat down to play. Beginner understudies are regularly encouraged to practice less, yet more frequently. Rather than arranging a mind-boggling hour or hour and a large portion of a couple of times seven days, make do with 15 minutes every day. The more reliable you are, the better you'll advance with your musical preparing. Apparently, on the off chance that you can deal with accomplishing over 15 minutes per day you are positively urged to do as such - however, the brilliant guideline is that it is smarter to practice for a little measure of time yet all the time.

#4. You go for the best quickly. Once more, learning music - regardless of whether you choose to figure out how to play the piano, the guitar, the flute or some other instrument - takes some time. Numerous piano beginners have this one song that they've heard on the radio, on the TV or at a show that made them need to play the instrument. In any case, it is essential not to skirt important steps basically because you are keen on learning that song. If an arithmetic educator were to tell you the best way to determine a variable based math condition before showing you the best way to duplicate and separation numbers, you'd unquestionably raise your hand and call attention to that you don't have the devices or information to fathom this sort of condition right now. The equivalent runs with playing piano: you can't play hard pieces until you have the apparatuses and the learning essential to comprehend those pieces. Try not to surge your education - go step by step and adapt gradually. Before you know it, you'll contain sheet music, realize how to put your hands on the piano and will be a couple of steps nearer to having the capacity to play that one song!

Piano For Beginners Guide

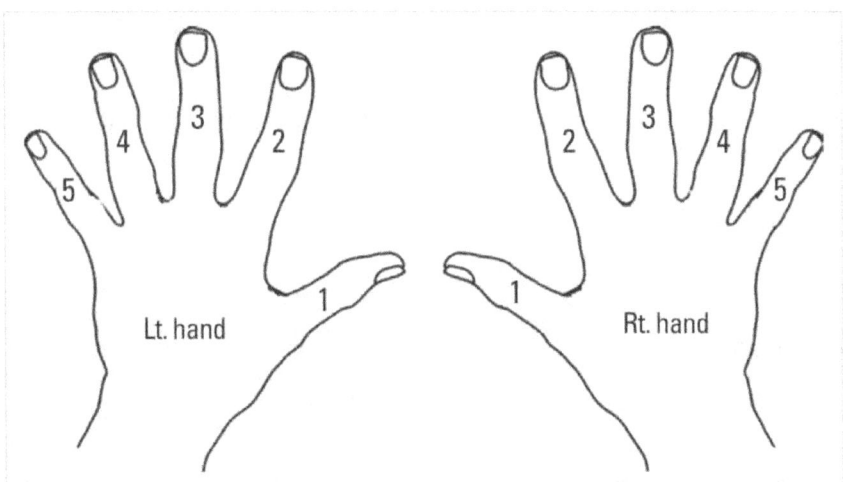

There are numerous ways to play piano for beginners, contingent upon your ability level, age, musical fitness, time accessible and objectives. This guide will enable you to decide your goals and locate a piano course or method dependent on your necessities.

Catchphrase for Beginners

As a rule, piano students fall under one of these types:

a) The piano is a diversion; I merely need to learn some simple songs and have a fabulous time

b) I don't have any desire to try perusing notes and play piano by ear

c) I need to achieve not too bad piano abilities regardless of whether it takes me at minimal longer

d) I need to study music genuinely, and I'm willing to set aside enough practice time

In case you're a type an) or b) student, you can show yourself piano utilizing one of the methods we suggest all through this site, and it would be dependent upon you to have an educator periodically for more direction and input. A great many people going on the web to get data on piano for beginners need to learn piano without anyone else.

Some piano learning projects practice on showing utilizing famous and additionally contemporary songs, others on playing by ear, and so forth. Locate the best one appropriate for your student type.

If you're a c) type student, at that point you could begin with a good course you can pursue, and as your piano playing enhances, you ought to consider periodic lessons to clean your abilities and right some negative behavior patterns, you may create.

At long last, in case you're a type d) student, you could begin with one of these projects, yet authoritatively are going to require the direction of a music instructor.

Utilizing a good piano method can supplement your piano guidance.

Beginner Piano Lessons

When are you one of the individuals who begin taking piano for beginners however got frustrated and quit? You presumably adopted the wrong strategy or were not practical about your musical objectives. If your piano learning background is exhausting, is because possibly you're in the incorrect classification from the ones referenced above, or you're following an old method that it is sufficiently challenging to comprehend and fun enough to pursue.

Sheet Music for Beginners

Did you realize that a portion of the fresher piano for beginners courses use prevalent and additionally contemporary songs? Did you know there are sites where you can get FREE sheet music for beginners? On these destinations, you'll discover songs from your most loved entertainers, motion pictures, established or occasional songs.

The Internet offers you better than ever ways to learn piano or console. Today there are some inventive frameworks where you can learn through pictures, recordings, and other visual guides. These cutting edge piano for beginners courses use the most recent innovation which enables you to learn songs quicker, less demanding and have a great time.

Piano For Beginners - Why Study Piano?

There are numerous excellent musical instruments — everyone has its character and style. Learning to play any of them is fulfilling and pleasant. So for what reason would somebody pick the piano over another instrument? For what reason would somebody choose a keyboard for beginners course finished, state, a tuba or woodwind class?

There are bunches of motivations to study piano. In the first place, it is a standout amongst the most differing instruments in Western music. A piano player can play practically any style of music. Hardly any devices have that much range. Who at any point knew about jazz oboe or blues bassoon? However, a piano can be played in established, pop, shake, jazz, and gospel styles, and considerably more.

The piano is polyphonic, giving it a wealth that most instruments don't have. By "polyphonic," I imply that you can, and ordinarily do, play more than one note at a time. In further developed piano music, the player plays chords instead of single notes. Although music composed for piano for learners may not utilize harmonies for each hand, tenderfoots' music is so far composed for all of the opposite sides to make music openly and in concordance. The two voices of a piano piece, the voice wrote for the right hand and the voice written for the left, bring a multifaceted nature of the sound that is unattainable in different instruments.

The piano can be played as a performance instrument, or to go with voice or another device, or as a component of a band or ensemble. So concerning courses of action and arrangement, a piano is flexible such that numerous musical instruments are most certainly not. Solo tympani, anybody?

Piano trains a starting musician such that different instruments don't. It requires a lot of manual ability since a piano player should almost certainly use each finger of two hands-frees. Indeed, even piano for beginners needs a musician to most likely peruse both the treble clef and the bass clef all the while. Also, working with chords and the two distinct voices played by the two different hands prompts a comprehension of music hypothesis and chord development that most different instruments don't offer.

Of course, there are noteworthy disadvantages to picking the piano. To express the self-evident, keyboards are enormous, overwhelming and confusing to move. Though a musician can get her instrument and convey it with her, a piano player can't go with hers. Indeed, even a second-hand piano can be very costly. Furthermore, some littler homes or condos are ill-suited for the significant bit of gear that even a little keyboard is.

Electronic keyboards can offer an option in contrast to acoustic pianos. Little, compact and generally modest, electronic keyboards can, at least, give away to a student to traverse the "piano for beginners" stage and learn proper fingering and how to peruse music. Regardless of the way that they don't have the sound quality that a piano has, a console can be the right decision in homes in which a keyboard isn't possible.

At last, the genuine motivation to play the piano is because the keyboard is lovely. Superb, creamy and with a convention of writing unmatched by most different instruments, even an upright piano is, well, amazing. Any eventual musician who is attempting to choose what device to take would settle on an incredible decision by picking a keyboard.

Piano For Beginners

I should need to familiarize you with the diverse methods used for preparing the piano for beginners. The main thing that would likely ring a bell is that you need to learn every individual note. To begin with, this variant was to instruct beginners where each letter is, learning to sight read the music and timeless reiterations. This is a very time devouring procedure and students, for the most part, need quite a while and a lot of lessons to almost certainly play the piano on the off chance that they don't lose intrigue and quit before they succeed playing the piano.

The second and quicker method is learning to play chords as opposed to learning the individual notes. Along these lines, the students of beginners for piano have a fabulous time because it is leaving and pleasant while preparing to play the piano. For students that need to play songs (and most are), this method is the better and quicker way and more exciting than to learn scales. Students can regularly learn to play songs inside their initial couple of lessons, and this manufactured certainty. Guitar players additionally use chord playing.

You additionally can choose to begin playing around with the piano and instruct yourself merely. It very well may be of extraordinary help becoming accustomed to the keyboard before going to classes, yet remember that a portion of the universes best musicians showed them self.

In the second spot, I might want to discuss available classes for students for piano for beginners. The most genuine students would typically experience universities, colleges and school programs where they would likewise be shown the historical backdrop of music and musical instruments. Some would also go for individual one-on-one classes to learn the piano. However, aggregate levels are similarly as good. The main drawback of gathering courses is the absence of opportunity to prepare when they suit you. Teachers for piano for beginners can be found in neighborhood indexes, and a visit to your nearby music store may control you into the correct heading. With the improvement of the web, there are courses accessible online that is exceptionally extraordinary, and more affordable, and is another incredible way for students to learn how to play the piano.

Finally, whatever you choose to do, it would be a good plan to complete estimation of the expense of the preparation, your extra time accessible and the capability of the teacher. With this stated, take as much time as necessary on choosing, and good fortunes playing the piano.

Digital Piano Keyboards

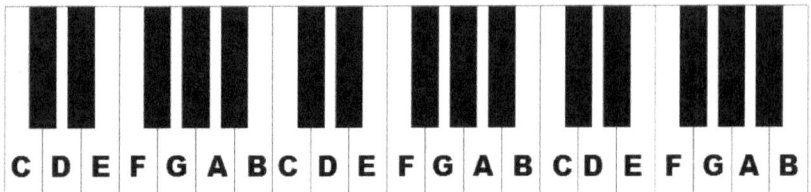

Digital Piano Keyboards are generally little in size contrasted with the acoustic piano. Typically they have keys from 20 to 88 cores and 4-5 octaves to 8-9 octaves. The vast majority want to purchase this as they are versatile and they have diverse varieties or can say changes of sounds.

The keys are littler contrasted with the acoustic piano which makes the treatment of the keys less demanding. This instrument likewise involves negligible space compared with the acoustic Piano, and they additionally come in various sizes appropriate for any distinctive individual. Contrasted with the acoustic Piano the Digital Piano is shoddy and it empowers one to utilize a USB association with an interface with a computer and here and there even the MIDI organization to associate with the network.

In a Digital Keyboard one needs to see to specific things which are a need as it is exorbitant. We should check the instrument altogether before paying for it. Things like the speaker, harmonies, sound control, outer harmonies, the volume control, earphones ought to likewise check the elements of each key as some keys may not work legitimately, so ensure you play and see all the keys and the crucial catches. Some shabby quality Pianos will, in general, have an absence of positive off notes, they may have even the rhythm issue so observe to that what you purchase merits the cash you pay. There is no damage in paying some more for the best quality and a since quite a while ago kept going.

There are numerous fabricates in the market, in particular, Casio, Yamaha, Roland, Korg, Kawai, Suzuki, Ketron, Kurzweil, Gem, and so forth. The Casio is the first and practical, and the Roland Company is the best among the Digital Piano Keyboards. Yamaha is said to be the most well-known. Korg is supposed to be on the higher end and are less expensive yet don't have the quality of Yamaha or Roland. Kawai Keyboards are light weighted and has an excellent sound impact. Diamond Keyboards are exceptionally, yet they do not have the quality and sound execution. Ketron Keyboards are considerably more, yet they are great. Suzuki does not have a high quality. Kurzweil likewise has a decent sound impact.

The has six points of interest contrasted with the acoustic piano, which are, the Digital Piano keyboard is moderate by numerous individuals as the acoustic is exceptionally exorbitant, the Piano keyboard is convenient, it has different sound assortments like we can play the harmonica, guitar, drums, strings, vibraphones, bass, and so on. The Digital Piano Keyboard has a MIDI or USB office to associate with the computer. There is no unsettling influence for the neighbors as one can utilize the earphones and tune in to their play lastly and most importantly the Digital Piano keyboard does not require tuning of the keys as it is digital there is zero chance of the tune setting changing however the acoustic piano need tuning to be done once in at regular intervals.

At long last, the contrast between the Digital Piano and the acoustic piano is that the acoustic Piano has sleds and strings to play. Exactly when the keys are pressed the vehicle hits the ropes to play the sound which postpones the sound timings yet in a Digital Piano Keyboard has a sensor which is digital, and the sounds are transmitted utilizing an intensifier and speakers, and you can control the volume level from low to high.

Piano Keyboards to Keep You Playing - What to Look For in a Keyboard

When searching for another keyboard, consider the name brand producers of piano keyboards. Take a gander at your financial plan and after that go from that point. Does that financial plan enable you to look at a portion of the debut producers out there? Does your business plan expect you to run with a lesser-known producer?

A portion of the names in piano keyboards are Korg, Kurzweil, Roland, Yamaha, Kawai, and Moog. There are a large group of others also, some with a full model line accessible. Check every producer's items from low-end to top of the line and look at crosswise over organizations for features advertised. In some cases, a lower-valued model may suit you similarly just as a higher-evaluated one that has numerous additional devices you may never utilize. The primary concern is to ensure any model you pick has an unmistakable, full sound looking like as close as conceivable a customary piano sound. You don't need a tinny sound that is more irritating than satisfying.

If you base your choice exclusively on cost, examine customer reports and item audits that may alarm you to item imperfections. You may locate some expensive models get awful press than lower-evaluated makes. Notwithstanding, don't give a piano keyboard a chance to buy blow your financial plan. You can generally overhaul not far off.

One critical thought when purchasing a piano console is the guarantee. In case you're purchasing another brand, ensure the warranty is appropriate with no unsuitable "aside from" provisions. In case you're buying utilized, endeavor to purchase from a merchant who offers even a six-month guarantee on a used item. They're out there; you merely need to search for them.

Consider the kind of keys your fingers will keep running crosswise over when you take a gander at piano keyboards. Do you need customary weighted keys that have the vibe of an acoustic piano? Do you need to contact delicate keys that spring energetically with minimal descending weight? Both are accessible, and looking at them will guarantee that it suits your touch. I would unquestionably suggest that you get both of these features, so your keyboard sounds as well as feels like an ordinary acoustic piano.

Think about whether you need an entire 88-key piano or one with fewer keys. It relies upon what you intend to play, the amount you need to spend, and the space you have in a room. You would prefer not to feel cramped with a keyboard whose length scarcely fits into a little place. Then again, if you plan on improving in a rush, at that point get an 88 key keyboard from the beginning so you won't need to stress over exceeding it.

Something else to consider in a piano keyboard is the number of controls a model has for sound alteration. Numerous consoles come outfitted with settings to make the piano sound like distinctive musical instruments. Some likewise have voice settings, so specific keys sound like a choir singing. Again, in case you need only your normal piano sound, you may not require all these sound controls. To minimize your costs, it's best to purchase a model with just the features you will utilize.

An important consideration, mainly if you live in a loft or apartment suite, is sound control. You need a keyboard that enables you to set the volume as low as could reasonably be expected while keeping up quality and purity of sound. You likewise need a keyboard that takes into account the earphone module, so you can play as noisy as you need without aggravating anybody.

With the present "becoming environmentally viable" concerns, you might need to research the vitality utilization of keyboards. Keyboards that are green agreeable are sure to be the most recent models and can spare you dollars on vitality bills. With that additional cash, you can move up to a higher-estimated keyboard later.

Extra things to consider are any unique advantages or rewards for purchasing. Some music studios move keyboards and may offer exercise or music book limits for buying from them. Some music stores offer music exercises on premises and may provide free basic piano exercises with a keyboard buy.

The last thing to think about when acquiring a keyboard is its ability for connections. Besides the earphones (and you'll need them without a doubt so you can practice quietly), you may need outlets for an enhancer or a Musical Instrument Digital Interface outlet. This enables you to guide a keyboard into a computer. The laptop likewise must have MIDI info. If your computer doesn't, you need to purchase a USB MIDI connector. With the best possible programming program set up, you can play notes on a keyboard and have them appear as composed music on your screen. The computer performs the records back, and the program stores the played notes on the computer. If this resembles an appealing choice, look for a keyboard with this outlet.

CHAPTER TWO

7 Reasons Why Digital Piano Keyboards Make Great Gifts

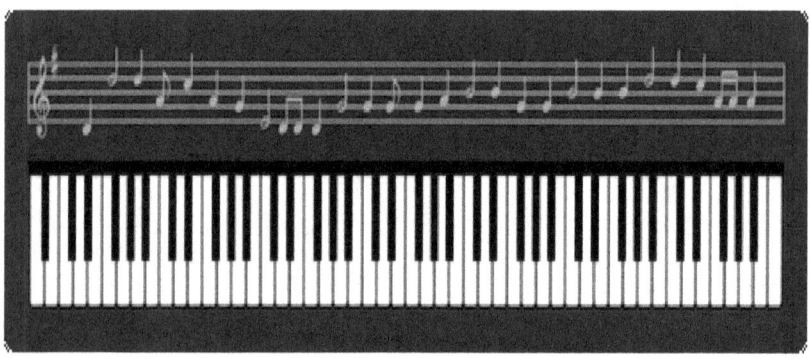

There is no uncertainty that a gift of music is a gift that continues giving since it can prompt a lifetime of delight and happiness. Figuring out how to play the piano is adequately trying for anybody, and provides a consistent feeling of accomplishment and fulfillment. Digital Piano keyboards, particularly the 88-key assortment, are extraordinary for birthday events, Christmas or gift-giving occasions of any sort, and here's the reason...

1. Estimate - They give the sound of a show grand piano in a little portion of the space. Genuine, you can get bureau models that resemble furniture and weigh to such an extent, yet a large part of the instruments sold are piece models - around five or six inches high and twelve or eighteen inches down. You can put them on a table best or spot them on a little stand, usually sold independently.

2. Lightweight - With a load of around thirty pounds or less, digital pianos are compact and effectively moved from spot to put. While they aren't as versatile as a guitar or a woodwind, they can travel effectively with other band gear and can be set up and brought down rapidly. They can even be conveyed in a gig pack and gone up against extended get-aways to keep in practice.

3. Musical voices - Digital piano keyboards can play the sounds or voices of numerous different instruments. It isn't strange to locate a digital piano that can play the sounds of a harp, organ, vibraphone, woodwinds, guitar, drums, and numerous others. The excellence of having every one of these sounds accessible is that it makes the practice sessions impressively additionally fascinating for the understudy. So on the off chance that you, your child or your little girl are figuring out how to play, having the capacity to change from a piano sound to harpsichord or an organ shields your practice from getting to be dull and monotonous - both for the one learning and the ones tuning in.

4. Recording capacity - With numerous digital pianos, you can record the music as its being played. In a few instruments, you can register at least two layers of music that would then be able to be consolidated to make the last account. This opens up another dimension of experimentation and happiness.

5. MIDI component - fresher instruments bolster the Musical Instrument Digital Interface (MIDI). With a MIDI component you can exchange music to a PC, and with unique programming, you can change over your music into printed sheet music. By a similar token, you can translate printed sheet music into the PC and play it back on the instrument. This gives you another approach to gain from and appreciate the apparatus.

6. Quiet playing - Almost all more current instruments accompany earphone abilities that let the understudy practice unobtrusively. Many have abilities for two arrangements of earphones so the music can be imparted to another person, still without upsetting the exercises of everyone around them.

7. Esteem - One last imperative motivation behind why digital piano consoles make extraordinary endowments is their generally ease in connection to their capacities. At the point when the expense of a digital piano is contrasted with the proportionate acoustic instrument, it indeed eclipses the acoustic regarding worth and value execution.

You can pay much more, obviously, yet an extremely decent advanced piano can be had for somewhere in the range of $400 and $800 US.

With everything taken into account, if you know somebody who plays piano or who has an enthusiasm for figuring out how to play, the digital piano console makes a truly reasonable blessing.

Eight Precious Tips to Help You Learn Piano by Yourself

Piano as an instrument is a moving enjoyment to play. For a few people, it is a concealed side interest and for about an inducing vocation. Be it any motivation to lay your hands on the piano; presently it is conceivable to end up great without long stretches of practice in costly piano exercises however at the solace of your home. With the basic knowledge of piano notes, keys, chords, and part of training one can self-train oneself towards turning into an ace musician.

Along these lines, presently you have chosen to let it all out alone, here I will walk you through some basic pointers to consider:

1. The decision between piano or keyboard to begin with for a fledgling:

The best and reasonable approach to start is Electronic Keyboards. The keyboard ought to be with 88 weighted keys. The weighted keys assemble hand quality and react progressively like the keys of an acoustic piano. Most electronic keyboards don't have weighted keys. On the off chance that a keyboard with 88 weighted keys is still out of your value to extend, we suggest that understudies utilize a keyboard with something like 61 keys.

2. Acclimate oneself with basic piano knowledge:

Can be either 88 keys digital piano or 61 keys advanced piano. More often than not for a fledgling, 61 keys piano keyboard is sufficient to cover the most extreme number of songs. Cores are composed in a particular 12-note design that rehashes over the whole piano key format. White piano keys are called naturals since they make a personal note when squeezed. Dark piano keys are called accidentals since they make a sharp or level note when compressed. There are seven naturals on the keyboard to be specific C-D-E-F-G-A-B.

3. Tutoring yourself with significant keys and chords

Begin with playing and acclimating to separate the tones, for example, the center tones (center of a piano), level tones (left dark keys), sharp tones (right dark keys), bass tones (low sounds) and high tones (high sounds) by listening to them. The premise step is to contemplate the eight unique keys and to recognize the sound everyone makes most likely. Songs are for the most part made out of a variety of chords, and the harmonies are made out of same notes. Distinguishing these notes is the significant advance towards recognizing a song. Concerning starter, one should center in getting acclimated with the basics chords, its area in the keyboard and it is sound.

4. Notice the examples

All songs are made out of musical examples. Chords rehash themselves often in a consistent beat or musicality. On the off chance that you can recognize the patterns that you hear, it is a lot less demanding to play a song that you understand. You'll have the capacity to realize which chords are joined with others.

5. Acing finger position

To honestly play, one needs to know with which fingers to play the keys. Following any instructional video or book pursue the example of numbering the fingers. With practice, one can ace the finger arrangement.

6. Utilize different instructional books and web

You can utilize instructional books and online destinations like You-tube as your mentors to figure out how to read music, play basic scales, chord movements, and afterward simple songs.

7. Practice is the key to progress

Play with sheet music to improve at sight reading, fingering and playing. Plan on rehearsing around three to four times each week for about a half hour trying not to proceed onward to the following exercise until you've aced the past use. Listen to songs. At that point, practice murmuring them and check whether you can copy the song on your piano or keyboard. Or then again, select a song that you like and utilizing the methods that you've learned, endeavor to play it by ear. Turning into a decent piano player requires loads of practice. You'll have to practice something like three times each week

8. Last however not the least; you can likewise go for online coaches

Since it is an expensive issue, for extra help for tuning up your basic knowledge one can likewise select online piano exercises. Utilizing this strategy close by would enable you to dodge negative behavior patterns which are hard to unlearn.

Fantasies to keep an eye for before beginning:

- Figure out how to read music is the sole method to gain proficiency with a piano

- Everything isn't just about the situation of fingers

- Rehearsing a solitary song more than once

- What are you hanging tight for! Tune up your piano and have a fabulous time playing!

Ten Reasons to Get Those Ten Fingers Playing Piano

To the individuals who love music, there are numerous reasons to play any instrument. The wide assortment managed us to look over is the thing that makes music unendingly charming. Picking any device to ponder is undoubtedly a beneficial undertaking.

One instrument features explicitly all that is awesome and delightful about music. It's lavishness of sound and the scope of musical notes it gives one to play make it an ageless inventive device. That instrument is the piano. Setting out on an investigation of this 88 fundamental enjoyment can give one a lifetime of cheerful encounters.

The piano is stunning in the two its multifaceted nature and straightforwardness. The musical note mixes authors compose for it, and players play on it, are unending. Nonetheless, the piano's component is essential. When you press a key on a keyboard, you cause a felt secured mallet to strike steel strings. The strings vibrate, and the vibrations transmit using a scaffold to a sounding board. This board couples the acoustic vitality to the air, and we hear everything as sound.

The sound from the piano makes it a standout amongst the most famous musical instruments on the planet.

Alongside its continuing sound, there are numerous different reasons everybody ought to figure out how to play music on the piano. Here are ten of them:

You Learn to Play Chords

A few instruments enable you to play single notes. They don't allow you to play chords. Chords are a lot of at least two distinct notes that sound at the same time. The piano, similar to the guitar, takes into consideration this chord playing. This implies you can advance a song with rich harmonies to go with the melodic line.

You Learn to "Hear" Chords

Perceiving the sound of chords is artistry in itself. Figuring out how to recognize chord sounds is gainful with regards to learning spontaneous creation not far off. Observing chord sounds will enable you to apply proper tune in a song as you improvise.

You Learn Variation

Concentrate piano will show you original song and chords. As you build up your aptitudes, you will figure out how to fluctuate these components in tune. You will do this on the fly as in the previously mentioned improvisational playing. You will likewise figure out how to modify songs on paper with these varieties. This is the place you explore different avenues regarding music composing. You will take an original melody and change it as indicated by your interpretation of the piece.

You Learn Eye-Hand Coordination

Simply watch somebody intently at the piano. You will see the interchange of eyes and turns in synchronization as they play. Concentrate the piano will encourage you to facilitate what you see on the keyboard with your engine aptitudes.

You Learn Left-Hand, Right Hand Coordination

You will build up this coordination from the get-go. Indeed, even with simple songs, this will happen. Your right hand will play single note songs, while your left-hand play basic chords. You need to get these two cooperating appropriately, so the song sounds satisfying.

You figure out how to Read Notes in the Lower and Higher Registers.

You will improve as a music reader when you gain proficiency with the piano. You will figure out how to read notes written in the lower registers, for example, the bass clef. You will likewise gain proficiency with their partners in the higher records, similar to the treble. What's more, you will figure out how to read these in the meantime, expertise itself.

You, Will, Learn to See Music as a Complete Whole

Playing music on the piano gives you a chance to see the entire structure of a song. A trumpet player, for instance, reads and represents the melodic line of the treble clef. That is typically the extent of the music before the person in question. A piano player sees chords, song, different clefs. Piano music has the entire of a song on paper, not only components of it.

It's a Great Accompaniment Instrument

This current one's direct. Each band can utilize a piano player. Glance around and perceive what number of piano players discover work with gatherings. They're popular.

It's a Great Solo Instrument

The piano is an instrument that offers much when heard individually. Most likely, different instruments sound great solo. In any case, the keyboard is just quite a lot more. It delivers a rich, full sound one of a kind onto itself. This is a direct result of its capacity to play song and agreement together; single notes and chords.

Energizes Audience Participation

A piano is understandable old useful for having a decent time. It, similar to the guitar, is incredible for get-together individuals around. It advances the blend of music playing with singing.

If you need to start an investigation of music, think about the piano. You will make the most of its flexibility and its capacity to play any musical style. The over ten reasons are ideal ones for getting your ten fingers playing, today.

Learn to Play Piano - Left-Hand Playing Is The Reverse of Right-Hand Playing

Playing piano requires two hands to play in the meantime at two distinct regions of the console, the right hand the mid to high range notes and the left side the bass notes.

To separate the two territories of the piano console to be played with each hand, music is composed of two arrangements of five lines. The above method of five lines is the spot that the right-hand notes are put. The lower five tracks are the place the records for the left hand are set.

To affirm the two arrangements of lines are for the higher registers and the lower enlists a sign is set on the most far left of each method of lines. The poster is known as a clef. The chef for the best arrangement of lines is the treble clef. The chef for the lower set of lines is the bass clef.

The fingers of the hands are numbered, from the thumbs of two sides being number 1 to the little digits being number 5. With the right hand, the thumb begins the lower notes and the fingers 2, 3, 4, and 5 play the signs to the right (logically higher in pitch) successively. The left-hand fingers play the contrary way. The thumb represents the more top pitch notes and other fingers moving left down the console play the lower pitch notes.

Music dependably has lower pitched notes at the base of the lines, and higher pitched notes at best. This remaining parts consistent paying little mind to the arrangement of lines being utilized. (Treble or Bass clef)

Perplexity can happen when initially endeavoring to play with the left hand. The notes on the music for the two clefs pursue similar principles of lower bills at the base and higher bills at best. The right hand continues the records with the huge thumb playing lower notes and the minor little finger playing the top notes. The left side does everything in turn around. The large inch represents the higher notes, and the small little finger plays the deep, overwhelming notes.

Music notes are named after the initial eight signs of the letter set, which is A to G. To almost certainly work out the records to be played, working the letters in order from A to G is simple; in any case, few of us gain proficiency with the message set in reverse. To pursue music, it is fundamental to know the letters in order from G to A. To play with the left hand; the capacity to understand the messages in order from G to A is pivotal as the left side plays its finger numbers in reverse. When this is aced with a little work on utilizing the left hand in reverse turns out to be second nature.

The most effective method to Play Piano - Both Hands at the Same Time

For some individuals when they start figuring out how to play the piano, one of the most challenging activities is planning two hands in the meantime. Having the capacity to simultaneously control both the left and right sides in the meantime is troublesome when we initially figure out how to play the piano. This is because the vast majority have a preferred hand. As a rule, the favored side is the right hand.

Factually it tends to appear a more significant number of individuals are right handed than left handed. So for a right-handed individual, the left hand will be the flimsier hand. As far as being feeble, I mean it doesn't move as quick, and the fingers aren't as deft. The muscles on the left hand will be increasingly slow because we won't utilize it as much as the right. Because of this more fragile left hand, learner piano players battle with playing the piano with two sides in the meantime.

Having the capacity to figure out how to play the piano with two hands requires lots of training. With lots of practice, the left side can be produced to represent similarly just like the right. With a lot of tolerance and devotion to adapting, each piano player can, in the end, learn and ace playing with two hands simultaneously.

To ace the strategy of playing with two hands in the meantime, you have to approach rehearsing the right way. When you first play a piano piece, you ought to figure out how to play with each hand separately in the wake of becoming accustomed to playing independently with two sides. Have a go at playing a couple of notes of the piano piece with two teams. Begin off with one note first and advancement to an ever-increasing number of records. Possibly have a go at playing a couple of bars of the piano piece with two hands. Gradually, yet definitely you will begin to create aptitudes that enable your hands to play together.

It may take a couple of long stretches of training, however, what is a couple of hours in an individual life or even multi-day. Try not to surrender and consistently work on playing piano pieces with two hands. Make sure to play with each side separately when you motivate another piano piece to play. Inevitably you will most likely play new melodies with two hands moderately rapidly.

Playing the scales with two hands in the meantime is another method for showing yourself how to play the piano with two sides. Figuring out how to play the piano with two hands sounds long and monotonous. The prizes of taking it moderately and figuring out how to play the piano more altogether are huge. Keep in mind not to race into things, and every beneficial thing requires some investment. When playing the scales make sure, to begin with, the right hand first as it were. Proceed onward to rehearsing with your left. At that point consolidate two sides together in the meantime.

As you get progressively alright with playing the scales with two hands, you can have a go at expanding the beat. You have to make sure to utilize a metronome to monitor what rhythm you are playing.

As you practice to an ever increasing extent, you will play with two hands effectively. Your muscle memory would have enabled you to play the piano with two hands without you notwithstanding pondering it. It will resemble your hands are on autopilot.

All in all, figuring out how to play the piano with two hands isn't hard. With lots of tolerance, determination and heaps of training you will play the piano with two sides in no time. Try not to surrender when troubles arise, push through the tough times and be rewarded over the long haul. Anybody can figure out how to play piano with two hands. Give it a go today and continue rehearsing.

Step by step instructions to Play Piano - Improve Hand Coordination.

Figuring out how to play piano necessitates that piano player to learn numerous aptitudes and procedures. These attitudes and methods take a long time of training when such ability to know is having incredible hand coordination.

What precisely is hand coordination with regards to playing the piano? It is how facilitated those hands are when playing with two sides in the meantime. A great many people think that its simple to play the scales with one side at a time. With regards to playing with two hands, the left hand and right hand don't appear to get along.

We can build up our hand coordination through a progression of activities. As we train increasingly more with these activities, our hand coordination ought to enhance, and we will be progressively sure about playing with two hands in the meantime.

The simple first exercise that you ought to figure out how to do is playing the scales and rehearsing each day until you are amazingly sure with them. Utilize just a single hand in your rehearsing and ensure you learn them all by heart. Practice till your fingers usually play absent much by way of reasoning going on in your mind.

In the wake of getting the scales all aced with private hands. Take a stab at staying them together and playing with two sides simultaneously. It will require some investment becoming accustomed to yet you ought to most likely gradually play the scales with two teams. Play slowly until you grow more certainty. As certainty expands, you can build your beat.

Making utilization of a metronome in your activities is a brilliant move. A metronome will enable you to keep your beat right as you are playing the piano.

First of all, you have to learn scales and practice these consistently, so discover some that you appreciate playing. Ensure you are sure of the notes, and where they are on the piano, so you have every one of the layers set up, if you are 100% of what you are doing hands separately, at that point when you set up your hands together it will be a lot simpler.

Another activity to attempt is playing a straightforward piece that requires two hands. Practice one bar at a time and play as moderate as you need. Try not to race into the following bar of the piece until you have aced every one of the bars previously hand. Learning things in pieces encourages you to adapt quicker.

Everybody learns at various velocities, so don't get excessively hard on yourself on the off chance that you don't prevail at first. Approach everything slowly and carefully, and it should merely click after some time. It's somewhat similar to scouring your stomach and applauding your head in the meantime. It requires practice for some, and you have to practice to become accustomed to the sentiment of utilizing two hands in the meantime.

The hardest thing that I find when playing with two hands is controlling the rhythm of the two sides. Both my hands attempt to play in a state of harmony which is an issue when a few pieces expect you to play out of the matchup. It requires investment to rehearse and with everything particular discipline brings about promising results.

Adhere to your course of action, and work on figuring out how to play the piano as much as you can. Figuring out how to play the keyboard is a lot of fun, and the enhancing hand coordination is very conceivable. Trust me, it is understandable. We weren't brought into the world realizing how to walk, and it took us lots of training and diligent work.

Taking everything into account, you can enhance your hand coordination after some time and figuring out how to play the piano is a lot of fun. Take as much time as necessary with all the fixings and put stock in yourself.
Everybody can figure out how to play the piano and you ought to trust that you can as well.

How to Play Piano - Playing With Both Hands Simultaneously

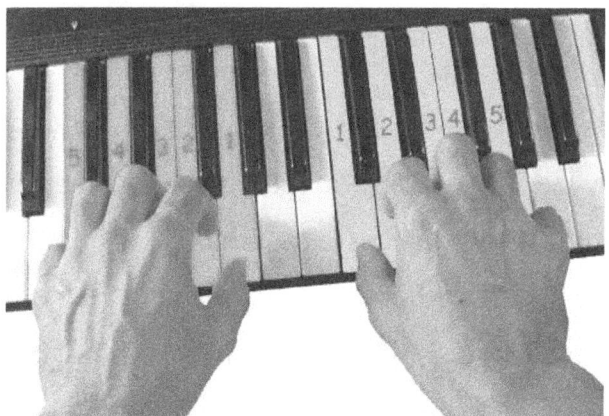

Playing with two hands sounds simple for a few, yet for some beginner piano players, it is hard and disappointing. Piano players get disappointed when they can't play something right. You see people play the piano with two hands and they make it look so natural. Well it isn't hard, and all beginner piano players need to realize how to play piano the right way, and it should work out quickly.

Through loads of training and diligent work of figuring out how to play piano, one can show themselves pretty much anything. Insights demonstrate that many individuals are more grounded in one hand than the other. Much of the time the piano player is more grounded on the right side.

A great many people are right-handed, and usually, their preferred hand moves much quicker than the other.

It isn't that the fingers in the hand can move quickly because they are fabricated unexpectedly, it is only that we have utilized less of the other side and are ungraceful in that non-preferred hand. For example, my left-hand plays the piano a tad slower than the right. It isn't that much slower, just marginally. I attempt ordinary rehearsing so that there isn't such a distinction.

When figuring out how to play piano with two hands at the same time, one must comprehend that it requires a touch of investment and tolerance. On the off chance that you don't have this, at that point forget about it. Make sure to rehearse. The primary thing I recommend is to play a piano piece that requires two hands with only the preferred side to begin with. At that point practice a similar article with the other hand. After a touch of training with two hands independently have a go at playing a bar of the piano with two sides.

Take one note at a time. Try not to surge it and merely play each note gradually. Play indeed steadily and ensure you are hitting the right notes with the right fingers. An incredible exercise to do before playing a piano piece with two hands will be to play the scales with two sides. Playing piano scales is an essential ability and ought to be continuously rehearsed.

Playing the piano scales with two hands gradually ought to be very simple. Accelerate as you show signs of improvement and play with a metronome. Remember about your stance and right-hand positions. Continuously keep the hand bent and play sitting up straight. Try not to slouch over and build up a terrible back.

With heaps of training, you can play a simple piano piece with two hands. Keep in mind that each learns at various velocities. Play gradually and increment the rhythm as you are showing signs of improvement. Through muscle memory, your hands will most likely play all the while without you considering it excessively.

All in all, figuring out how to play the piano with two hands isn't that difficult. With a touch of training, even the clumsiest of piano players can do it.

Step by step instructions to Play Piano With Both Hands - From Beginner To Professional

Figuring out how to play piano with two hands is a test for some piano players, from beginner to proficient. Notwithstanding for qualified piano veterans, a tune or musicality goes along that is trickier than usual when attempting to play with two hands on the piano.

Regardless of whether you're a beginner or propelled piano player, the most ideal approach to approach "hands together" issues on the piano is to separate the specific melody or section into sensible lumps for rehearsing, moderate down those lumps enough to play them, at that point develop the beat and set up the pieces back together.

Sounds simple, right? Perhaps not right now. However, my objective with this article is to tell you precisely the best way to do it.

In case you're a beginner, you might experience difficulty with some essential two-hand piano patterns, so we should investigate a couple that you can rehearse and that will sound incredible once you can play them.

We'll begin with my most loved shake and move pattern - how about we take a gander at the bass first.

In the left hand, rehash the accompanying pattern: C A G A, moving from C, down to A, down to G, at that point up to An, and back to C to begin once again. C A G A - C A G A. This is a 4-beat pattern regular in shake and moving bass lines.

In your right hand, shift back and forth between the accompanying two chords, utilizing center C and the other two notes directly over that C:

C E G C F A

In this way, in a 4-beat measure, you'll play:

1. C E G

2. C F A

3. C E G

4. C F A

Presently, play both those patterns together, and you ought to have an excellent sounding rock and move a piano line. To play with the right-hand musicality a bit, keep the left-hand bass line consistent on the 1 2 3 4 beats, yet begin to move the chords in the right hand a little off the pounds. For instance, you may take a stab at foreseeing the chord on beat one by playing it somewhere between hit 4 and beat 1.

To enable you to check, you should need to think about the beats as ONE-and-TWO-and-THREE-and-FOUR-and, which is fundamentally separating quarter note beats into eighth notes, on the off chance that you know a little about music as of now.

Presently, play the first chord on the "and" after the fourth beat, and hold it until it's time to play the music from beat 2 of the following measure. You can attempt other beat varieties, as well - let your ear be the judge for what sounds right.

How about we attempt somewhat more convoluted pattern - sort of a Latin vibe.

The left-hand bass is played on beats 1, 2 1/2 (the "and" of 2), 3, and 4 1/2 (the "and" of 4):

- C G C is played again and again. The two G's are represented exceptionally near one another, and the two C's are performed near one another.

- In the right hand, just play a C significant chord: C E G. Be that as it may, to make it intriguing, play it on the accompanying beats: 1, 2, 3 1/2, and 4 1/2, at that point hold the chord on beat 4 1/2 through beat 1 of the following measure, until it's time to play the music on hit 2 once more.

- It's somewhat difficult to clarify without composed music, yet check whether you can work out the pummels yourself and line the notes/chords for the right and left hands. This sort of activity will enable you to perceive two-hand piano patterns and improve at examining them yourself at whatever point you have to play them.

CONCLUSION

Facts About Famous Musicians

Frédéric Chopin

Frédéric Chopin Facts

1. Frederic Francois Chopin was born in Poland.
2. His birthday was March 1, 1809.
3. He spent most of his life in the two cities of Warsaw and Paris.
4. His father was French; his mother Polish.
5. At the age of nine he made his first public appearance as a pianist.
6. Many distinguished people welcomed him to Paris.
7. Among them were Liszt, Berlioz, Meyerbeer, Heine.
8. His first weeks in Paris were discouraging; his first concert poorly attended.
9. This tempted him to return to Poland.
10. But his friends urged him to remain in Paris.

11. Finally success came.

12. Chopin was described as one who spoke little, especially among strangers.

13. Some of the music forms which he wrote are the nocturne, waltz, mazurka, impromptu, concerto, polonaise, etude

14. Schumann was one of the first to declare Chopin a genius.

15. Chopin worked hard all his life.

16. But in his last years he suffered from ill-health.

17. Like Milton, Beethoven, Stevenson and Grieg, he kept on with his work, in spite of his illness.

18. Chopin once went to England and Scotland.

19. Chopin was very fond of Bach and urged his pupils to practice Bach pieces every day for the mental drill as well as the drill for the fingers.

Johann Sebastian Bach

1. Full name: Johann Sebastian Bach.

2. Born 1685, died 1750.

3. As a little boy he sang in the streets, begging from door to door.

4. His father and mother died when he was ten years old.

5. He went to live with his brother.

6. He took his first position when he was seventeen.

7. He used to walk long distances to hear famous organists, one of whom was named Buxtehude.

Wolfgang Amadeus Mozart

1. Full name: Wolfgang Amadeus Mozart.

2. Born Jan. 27, 1756; died Dec. 5, 1791.

3. The sister's name was Maria Anna.

4. Maria Anna was five years older than Wolfgang.

5. The pet names of the children were Wolferl and Nannerl.

6. Little Mozart loved to hear his sister play.

7. He started to study when he was four.

8. Mozart went on a concert tour with his sister when he was six years old.

9. When he was a child he visited many great cities, among them Paris, London and Vienna.

Ludwig van Beethoven

1. The composer's full name was Ludwig van Beethoven.

2. He was born at Bonn on the River Rhine. (Look for Bonn on the map.)

3. His birthday is December 16, and his birth year was 1770.

4. The Beethoven House is now a Museum.

5. Beethoven's father was a singer.

6. Ludwig began to study music at the age of four.

7. He was shy and quiet in school, always thinking even then of music.

8. Even as a little boy he composed music.

9. When he was ten years old his first published composition appeared.

10. A teacher who helped him very much was Christian Gottlob Neefe.

Joseph Haydn

1. He was born at Rohrau, in Hungary, March 31, 1732.

2. He was a few weeks younger than George Washington.

3. As a little boy he loved to hear his father and mother sing.

4. While they sang he played on a "make-believe" violin, of two sticks.

5. He left home at the age of six and never lived there again.

6. First he became a choir-boy at Hainburg.

7. When he was eight years old he entered St. Stephen's in Vienna as a chorister.

8. After he left St. Stephen's he worked hard for many years. Many people whom he met in this time helped him.

9. Among his friends of this period were: Metastasio, Porpora, Gluck, Mozart and his father, and Beethoven.

10. For a time he was Beethoven's teacher.

11. He spent a great part of his life in the Esterhazy family.

12. Here he was Vice-Capellmeister and composer to the Prince.

Edvard Grieg

1. Grieg was born June 15, 1843, near Bergen, Norway.

2. His father's ancestors were Scotch folk who went to Norway after the Battle of Culloden, in 1745.

3. It was Grieg's mother who gave him his first lessons.

4. One of his best friends--and one who did much for him-- was Ole Bull, the great violinist.

5. Grieg studied at the Leipzig Conservatory.

6. His teachers were Moscheles, Hauptmann (who liked his music), Richter, and Papperitz.

7. Sir Arthur Sullivan, who composed the opera, _Pinafore_, was one of Grieg's fellow students at Leipzig. Dudley Buck, the American composer, was there at the same time.

8. Among Grieg's friends were Gade, Nordraak, Ibsen, Bjornson and Svendsen.

9. He married his cousin, Mina Hagerup, who was a fine singer.

10. Grieg composed for the piano, voice, violin, and for the orchestra.

11. Grieg wrote music to Ibsen's _Peer Gynt_, at the poet's request.

12. The Norwegian Government granted Grieg a pension, so that
he could be free to devote himself to composition.

Robert Schumann

1. Robert Schumann was born at Zwickau, in Saxony, Germany, on June 8, 1810.

2. When Schumann was nine years old he heard the great pianist Ignaz Moscheles play and resolved to become a great pianist.

3. When Schumann was a youth he showed a gift for writing poetry.

4. Schumann's father was a successful book-seller.

5. All through his life Schumann was a great lover of the writings of the German author, Jean Paul (whose full name was Jean Paul Richter). Much of his music shows his high regard for that writer of fairy stories.

6. Schumann was twenty-one years old when he injured his hand and learned that therefore he could not hope to be a pianist. It was then that he made up his mind to be a composer.

7. Schumann had enough means to live in comfort. He was not poor, as were Mozart, Schubert, and some others.

8. Robert and Clara Schumann had eight children, and some of Schumann's best music was written to interest his children. 9. Schumann died July 29, 1856.

Richard Wagner

1. Richard Wagner wrote operas.

2. He was born May 22nd, 1813.

3. How long did Wagner study music?

4. His operas, like the novels of Charles Dickens, are full of wonderful characters.

5. Besides people of every day kind there are gods and goddesses, and giants, and other strange beings in his operas.

6. As a boy Richard Wagner went to a classical school.

7. He was always fond of music.

8. He could translate Greek when he was only thirteen years old.

9. Even as a little boy he said: I intend to become a poet.

10. He wrote plays and he read the plays of Shakespeare in English.

Giuseppe Verdi

1. Giuseppe Verdi was born in Roncole, Italy, October 10, 1813.

2. He began to learn the Spinet when he was seven years old.

3. The Spinet is an early form of the piano.

4. Among the great composers who were alive when Verdi was a little boy were: Beethoven, Schubert, Berlioz and Schumann.

5. He became organist at Roncole when he was ten years old (1823).

6. He went to school in Busseto and lived with a cobbler.

7. After a time he studied in Milan.

8. But not at the famous Milan Conservatory, for he was told there that he had no special talent for music.

9. Verdi wrote thirty operas.

10. The first was performed in 1839, when he was twenty-six years old.

CONCLUSION

When you have concluded that you might genuinely want to play the piano, at that point the principal thing that turns out to be clear, is how troublesome it indeed is. People have no clue the amount you need to figure out how to play the piano. For instance, you can play the piano alright with one hand, yet when you endeavor to do it with two sides, at that point, everything appears to be so difficult. How to play the piano with two hands?

Indeed, even the simple things in life can be troublesome, on the off chance that you are not doing them effectively and the hard stuff can be simple if you are doing the right things. Figuring out how to play a melodic instrument can be practically inconceivable on the off chance that you utilize the wrong strategies and loathe what you are doing.

The most severe issue is that people think that its exceptionally difficult to appreciate figuring out how to play the piano. If you are adhered and helpless to play piano with two hands, at that point you have two options, well really three decisions.

www.ingramcontent.com/pod-product-compliance
Lightning Source LLC
Chambersburg PA
CBHW062039120526
44592CB00035B/1615